To see more of our books, visit us at:
www.PuppyDogsAndIceCream.com

THE FANTASTIC WORLD OF
Monkeys & Apes
AND MORE

LEARN

FUN FACTS

SIZE

WEIGHT

LOCATION

AGES 3-10

Dr. Tara Stoinski, CEO of the
Dian Fossey Gorilla Fund

FUN FACTS
About Our Furry Friends

About the Author

Hello from the forests of Rwanda, home of the Dian Fossey Gorilla Fund and the gorillas we protect.

Of all the primates you'll read about in this book, **my favorite are gorillas**. I've been studying them for my entire career, and I'm fascinated by how they are like us in so many ways: they live in families, they laugh and play, they grieve when a family member dies, and they love to eat and take naps. They are also very smart - **we have observed gorillas dismantling traps set by poachers**!

But gorillas are just one of the hundreds of amazing types of primates. Primates include our closest living relatives - **chimpanzees and bonobos who share almost 99% of their DNA with us!** And they come in a huge array of shapes and sizes. A male gorilla can weigh up to 400 pounds while the Madame Berthe's mouse lemur weighs only 1.1 ounces. It would take 6,400 of them to equal one gorilla!

In this book you'll learn about **18 different types of primates**. Who knows? Maybe you'll agree with me that gorillas are the most amazing animals on the planet. Or maybe you'll fall in love with a different primate - they're all fascinating creatures with traits that make them unique. Tamarins and marmosets generally give birth to

twins and the whole family helps care for them, Japanese macaques like to sit in hot springs, chimpanzees use tools to fish for termites and ants, and lemurs are found only in Madagascar - just to name a few examples!

There is one thing that primates have in common: **They need our help to survive**. Because of habitat loss, poaching, and climate change, more than 60% of the estimated 300 primate species on earth are threatened with extinction in the wild.

Hopefully you'll finish the book with a newfound passion for primates, and you'll join us in our quest to ensure that their habitats stay safe and pristine. The organization that I run, the Dian Fossey Gorilla Fund, is the largest organization in the world dedicated fully to conserving gorillas and their amazing forest homes. Our trackers are in the forest every single day protecting individual gorillas and their families. We remove traps set by poachers that could injury or even kill a gorilla. The good news is that because of conservation efforts like these, **the number of some gorilla populations are increasing**.

I hope you enjoy learning more about some of the fascinating primates we are lucky to share the planet with. One of the best things you can do for them is to help share their stories. The more people understand how cool primates are, the more we hope they will want to help join the effort to ensure that they are around for many years to come!

Dr. Tara Stoinski
CEO of the Dian Fossey Gorilla Fund

Western Lowland Gorilla

Gorilla gorilla gorilla

FUN FACTS

Gorillas are the largest of the great apes.
We share about 98% of our DNA with gorillas.

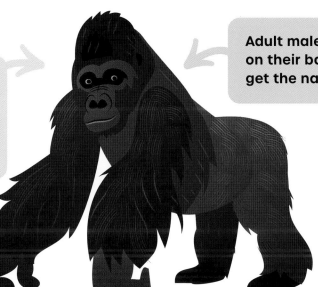

They are generally black in color with some gray mixed in and even red on the head

Adult males will have silver hairs on their back, which is how they get the name silverback

Gorilla nose shape and structure is unique and used by researchers to identify individuals

Where do they live?
Western Central Africa:
Gabon, Republic of Congo,
Cameroon, Equatorial Guinea

How big are they?
Male - 400 lbs, 5 ft
Female - 180 lbs, 4.5 ft
400 lbs = a lion

What do they eat?
Leaves, stems, shoots, fruit, and occasionally ants

Chimpanzee

Pan troglodytes

FUN FACTS

Chimpanzees are famous for using tools. They will insert sticks into termite mounds to "fish" out termites, or use balled-up leaves as sponges to soak up water to drink.

Faces are light when they are born but darken with age

The bare skin on their hands and feet give them a better grip to climb and use tools

Chimpanzees groom each other to keep clean and socialize

Where do they live?
Forested areas across Central Africa from Senegal to Tanzania

How big are they?
Male - 150 lbs, 4.5 ft
Female - 90 lbs, 4.5 ft
4.7 ft = a teenager

What do they eat?
Seeds, fruit, leaves, flowers, insects, bark, and will hunt monkeys and small mammals

Bonobo

Pan paniscus

FUN FACTS

Bonobos and chimpanzees are our closest living relatives. Unlike chimpanzees, bonobo society is matriarchal where females are dominant over males.

Bonobos are capable of laughing as a display of emotion and playful behavior

They are slightly smaller in size than chimpanzees, but have longer legs

They have dark skin on their face, hands, and feet

Bonobos are more comfortable walking upright than chimpanzees

Where do they live?
Democratic Republic of Congo

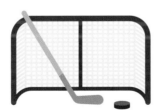

How big are they?
Male - 100 lbs, 4 ft
Female - 65 lbs, 4 ft
4 ft = a hockey net

What do they eat?
Leaves, stems, fruit, and insects

Patas Monkey

Erythrocebus patas

FUN FACTS

One of the few primate species adapted to living outside of the forest, they prefer savanna environments. Considered the fastest primate, they can run at speeds up to 35 mph.

They can store large amounts of food in their cheeks while foraging

They have a white tuft of hair around the mouth that resembles a mustache

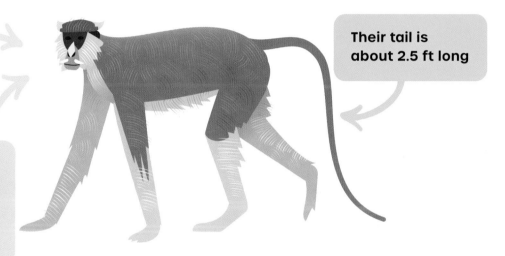

Their tail is about 2.5 ft long

Where do they live?
Savanna plains across central Africa

How big are they?
Male - 27 lbs, 5 ft
Female - 14 lbs, 4 ft
27 lbs = a medium dog

What do they eat?
Fruit, insects, leaves, roots, and bird eggs

Mandrill

Mandrillus sphinx

FUN FACTS

Mandrills are the largest monkeys, and one of the most colorful primates.

Male mandrills will lose color as they lose status in social groups

Males have vibrant colors of red, blue, and purple on their face with golden yellow beards and the more colorful they are the more attractive they appear

Males have red and blue butts to attract mates and be more visible in forests

Where do they live?
Cameroon, Gabon, and Republic of Congo

How big are they?
Male - 70 lbs, 3 ft
Female - 28 lbs, 2 ft
3 ft = a baseball bat

What do they eat?
Fruit, seeds, fungi, roots, insects, invertebrates, amphibians, and even small vertebrates

Gelada

Theropithecus gelada

FUN FACTS

Geladas are the only primate that is primarily a grass eater. More than 90% of their diet is grass.

Geladas are known as bleeding-heart baboons, defined by the vibrant red hourglass-shaped patch on their chest

Adult males have a long cape of brown and black hair that extends to their shoulders

Females have the hourglass, but it is much less pronounced

They have a reinforced butt that allows them to sit for a long time and forage grass

Where do they live?
High mountain meadows of Ethiopia

How big are they?
Male - 40 lbs, 4 ft
Female - 24 lbs, 3.5 ft
2 ft = a medium dog

What do they eat?
Grass and herbs

Hamadryas Baboon

Papio hamadryas

FUN FACTS

Hamadryas baboons were considered a sacred animal by the ancient Egyptians

Males have a distinctive mane of silvery hair

Females, which are half the size of males, lack the cape and are brown all over

They have very complex social structures as some groups can reach several hundred individuals

Where do they live?
East Africa and the Arabian peninsula

How big are they?
Male - 45 lbs, 2.5 ft
Female - 25 lbs, 1.5 ft
2.5 ft = 2 bowling pins

What do they eat?
Grass, seeds, fruit, roots, bird eggs, carrion, small mammals, and occasionally insects

Ring-Tailed Lemur

Lemur catta

FUN FACTS

Males engage in stink fighting, which involves rubbing oils from their scent glands on their tails and waving them at rivals.

Their "masked" face coloration resembles a raccoon

They have a super long and bushy tail with prominent black and white bands

Ring-tailed lemurs enjoy sunbathing

Where do they live?
Madagascar

How big are they?
5 lbs, 3.5 ft
3.5 ft = a baseball bat

What do they eat?
Leaves, flowers, insects, fruit, and even small vertebrates

Coquerel's Sifaka

Propithecus coquereli

FUN FACTS

Coquerel's sifakas are lemurs that move by leaping through the forest, covering expanses of up to 40 feet!

Their face is black and furless with a white patch of hair on the nose

They always start their day by basking in the sun before going out to forage

Their fur is mostly white with maroon patches on the chest, front of the thighs, and front of the arms

They love to hop sideways and like kangaroos while on the ground

Where do they live?
Madagascar

How big are they?
9-12 lbs, 3 ft

9-12 lbs = a bowling ball

What do they eat?
Leaves, flowers, and fruit

Aye-Aye

Daubentonia madagascariensis

FUN FACTS

They are the world's largest nocturnal primate. Their extra long middle finger is used to tap on wood and listen to the changing sound to detect insect tunnels. This technique is called percussive foraging.

Their large incisor teeth continually grow and help them penetrate wood to extract insects

Their large, round ears are specialized to detect the sound of moving grubs or larvae

Aye-ayes use their very long, skinny fingers to reach into small holes in trees and logs

Where do they live?
Madagascar

How big are they?
5 lbs, 3 ft
5 lbs = a chihuahua

What do they eat?
Larvae, insects, and fruit

Japanese Macaques

Macaca fuscata

FUN FACTS

Also known as snow monkeys, Japanese macaques are famous for using hot springs to bathe and warm up when the weather is cold.

Young Japanese macaques will roll up snowballs just for fun

Their fur is much thicker to keep them warm in snowy environments

They shed their thick winter coat in the summer when temperatures rise

Where do they live?

Japan

How big are they?

Male - 25 lbs, 2 ft
Female - 20 lbs, 2 ft
25 lbs = a car tire

What do they eat?

Plant leaves, flowers, fruit, and insects

Rhesus Macaques

Macaca mulatta

FUN FACTS

These monkeys are very mischievous and will break into homes to steal food. They also let other macaques know there is food using specific calls.

In India these monkeys are considered sacred and are even gifted food as offerings

These resilient and adaptable monkeys have the greatest geographic distribution of any nonhuman primate

They have adapted well to live in urban environments alongside humans

Where do they live?
Across South, Central, and Southeast Asia

How big are they?
Male - 17 lbs, 2.5 ft
Female - 12 lbs, 2 ft
2 bowling pins

What do they eat?
Leaves, fruit, insects, and roots

Red-Shanked Douc Langur

Pygathrix nemaeus

FUN FACTS

Considered to be one of the most colorful monkeys, the red-shanked douc langur is distinguished from other langur species by the beautiful color of hair on their legs.

Face is a dull yellow around the eyes, and a pale white around the mouth

Due to the range of colors on these monkeys they are sometimes referred to as "costume monkeys"

They have maroon-red fur on the front of their legs which leads to their name

These monkeys frequently burp while digesting their food

Where do they live?
Vietnam and Laos

How big are they?
Male - 23 lbs, 3.5 ft
Female - 18 lbs, 2.5 ft
23 lbs = a gold bar

What do they eat?
Young leaves, shoots, buds, seeds, flowers, and unripened fruit

Sumatran Orangutan

Pongo abelii

FUN FACTS

Orangutans are the heaviest tree-dwelling animal, and the arm span of a male can be over 7 feet. Females only reproduce every 8-9 years.

Males have very long and flowing reddish hair on their arms

Males have pads on the side of their face known as cheek pads or flanges

Arms are longer than their legs which helps with their arboreal lifestyle

Orangutans are skilled with tools to extract insects from holes in trees

Where do they live?
Sumatra

How big are they?
Male - 175 lbs, 4.5 ft
Female - 100 lbs, 4 ft
4.5 ft = a hockey net

What do they eat?
Ripe fruit, leaves, seeds, bark, flowers, honey, insects, and vines

White-Throated Capuchin

Cebus capucinus

FUN FACTS

They are very resourceful monkeys and can use sticks as weapons against predators like snakes.

They communicate through a wide range of facial expressions and vocal calls

Studies have shown they may use herbs as a form of medicine

Their tail is longer than their body

They are one of the most intelligent of the New World monkeys

Where do they live?
South America: Ecuador, Panama, and Colombia

How big are they?
Male - 9 lbs, 3.5 ft
Female - 6 lbs, 2.5 ft
9 lbs = a bowling ball

What do they eat?
Fruit and insects

Golden Lion Tamarin

Leontopithecus rosalia

FUN FACTS

They almost always give birth to twins, and the whole family helps to care for the infants, including older siblings.

Their lion-like mane and golden hair color give them their name

Juveniles like to playfully steal food from their parents

Their tails are longer than their bodies, but they are not prehensile

They use their long fingers to rip up tree bark to find insects

Where do they live?
Southeastern Brazil

How big are they?
1.2 lbs, 1.5 ft

1.2 lbs = a soccer ball

What do they eat?
Fruit, insects, and small invertebrates

Red Howler Monkey

Alouatta seniculus

FUN FACTS

Their call can be heard up to 3 miles away, and is used to defend their territory from other groups.

Their hyoid bone and enlarged larynx create a resonating chamber to amplify their calls

Due to their leafy diet, they spend much of the day resting

The bottom tip of the tail is hairless for better grip

They live in groups of 15-20 individuals

Where do they live?
Central and South America: Colombia and Bolivia

How big are they?
Male - 11 lbs, 3.5 ft
Female - 7 lbs, 3 ft
11 lbs = a bowling ball

What do they eat?
Leaves, fruit, nuts, and flowers

Geoffroy's Spider Monkey

Ateles geoffroyi

FUN FACTS

Their tail is prehensile, meaning it can act as a fifth limb, and support their full body weight. This allows them to move more quickly through the trees.

Sometimes called black-handed spider monkeys due to their characteristically black hands

Due to their long, grippy fingers, their thumb has been rendered functionless over time

They can hang from branches just by their tail

Long and slender limbs give them excellent mobility through the trees, and a spider-like appearance

Where do they live?
Central America: Mexico, Belize, and Costa Rica

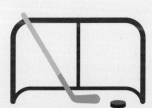

How big are they?
Male - 18 lbs, 4 ft
Female - 15 lbs, 3.5 ft
4 ft = a hockey net

What do they eat?
Ripe fruit, young leaves, flowers, buds, occasionally bark, nuts, seeds, insects, spiders, and eggs

CLAIM YOUR FREE GIFT!

Visit

PDICBooks.com/Gift

Thank you for purchasing
The Fantastic World of Monkeys & Apes,
and welcome to the
Puppy Dogs & Ice Cream family.

We're certain you're going to love
the little gift we've prepared for you
at the website above.